TO MR. GARY. LOVE, JULIA.
—JC

TO MY BOYS. TO BE CALLED "DAD" IS
A GIFT NO MONEY CAN EVER REPLACE.
—GG

THIS BOOK IS DEDICATED TO ALL
THE YOUNG SAVERS AND GIVERS.
—JC

Text © 2023 by Julia Cook and Garett Gunderson
Illustrations by Josh Cleland
Cover and internal art and design © 2023 by Sourcebooks
Sourcebooks and the colophon are registered trademarks of Sourcebooks.
This book was illustrated on the computer in Photoshop using a Wacom Cintiq tablet.
Published by Sourcebooks eXplore, an imprint of Sourcebooks Kids
P.O. Box 4410, Naperville, Illinois 60567-4410
(630) 961-3900
sourcebookskids.com
Cataloging-in-Publication Data is on file with the Library of Congress.
Source of Production: PrintPlus Limited, Shenzhen, Guangdong Province, China
Date of Production: April 2023
Run Number: 5030588
Printed and bound in China.
PP 10 9 8 7 6 5 4 3 2 1

I Am Money

WORDS BY JULIA COOK AND GARRETT GUNDERSON
PICTURES BY JOSH CLELAND

sourcebooks eXplore

I AM MONEY.

Some people like to think that I grow on trees...but I don't! If I did, I wouldn't be worth very much.

Turns out, I'm worth **A LOT**! If you have me, you can buy the **BASIC** things in life that everybody needs.

You can buy a purple houseboat with green shutters.

You can buy fuzzy patchwork pants.

SALE

You can buy some **PIZZA**!

And you can even buy a guinea pig if you want one!

AMAZING GUINEA PIG FOR SALE!

When it comes to the **BASICS**, I can make you happy. But no matter how hard I try...I can't make you happier.

I may be valuable, but your value in life has nothing to do with how much you can buy.

I wear a lot of different outfits.

These are my
old-school jackets.
I love how shiny they are.

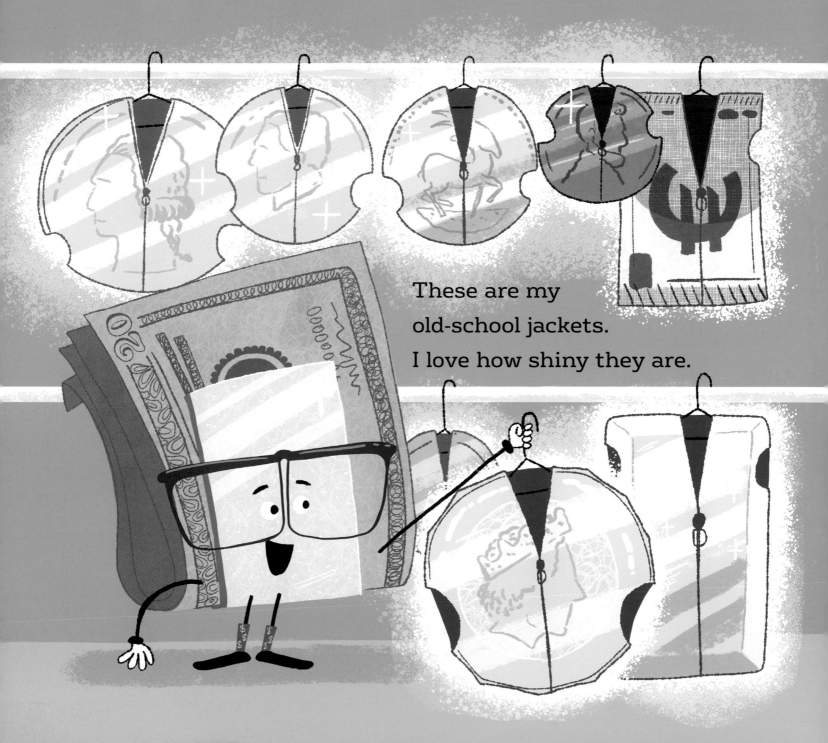

Sometimes I like to dress up in my digital and crypto clothes.

And these are my credit card coats. Once in a while, when I'm wearing them, they try to convince me to buy stuff that costs more money than I have!

This makes people happy at first, but then later, when they get the bill, they feel stressed out, worried, and sometimes sad.

There are four things all kids need to know about money.

HOW TO EARN ME

HOW TO SAVE ME

HOW TO SPEND ME

and most important of all...

MONEY 101

EARN

SAVE 15%

SPEND $

GIVE

HOW TO GIVE ME AWAY

There are a lot of ways to earn money.

You can mow lawns.

You can make a lemonade
stand and sell lemonade.

You can sing for people.

You can even let a banker or an investor use a part of me and lend it to others. You work hard to earn me, and if you're careful and smart about it, I can end up working for you! Now that's **INTEREST**-ing...

Every time you earn me, put some of me in your **SAVINGS JAR**. Use a clear jar. Some people like to put me inside of a dark pig. I don't like that because I can't see out and you can't watch me grow.

Saving money for a "rainy day" is important. Sometimes things can happen that we just don't plan on.

P.S. If you want to use me once in a while and it's not raining, that's OK too.

I love it when you spend me on things that you really want to buy.

Like purple bubble gum...

Or a bike horn...

Or a super-fantabulous light-up yo-yo...and even guinea pig stuff!

GUINEA PIG LAIR

HOW TO WIN FRIENDS and INFLUENCE GUINEA PIGS

But don't let me burn a hole in your pocket... I mean, if you waste me on things that you don't really want or need, I feel worthless.

My favorite thing that you can spend me on is **YOU**.

INVEST IN YOURSELF!

I am so happy when you use me to get better at the things you love to do.

I can pay for trombone lessons,

and art classes,

and zoo school!

Always keep in mind...

YOU ARE YOUR VERY BEST ASSET.

If you can become really good at what you love to do, you can make more of me than you will ever need. And then, you can do the coolest thing ever...

MONEY TIPS FOR YOU!

 You were born with gifts. Invest in yourself! Learn new things. Find out what you do best, and work hard to discover what you love to do. YOU are your GREATEST INVESTMENT!

 Your value in life has nothing to do with what you can or cannot buy.

 Money alone cannot make you happy. Using money to help others and improve yourself can help make you happy.

 Pay yourself first! For every dollar you get, put 15 cents away in a special place. This is a great money habit to have. Always remember to take care of yourself so you can give your best to others.

 Don't spend money that you do not have.

Spend your time discovering new things and building relationships with others. You may be only one relationship or idea away from learning, growing, and solving any problem.

 You can work for money, and your money can also work for you if you are a smart investor. Now that's INTEREST-ing.

 Some people are afraid to admit they don't know a lot about money. Of course, nobody knows everything. Get to know people who are good with money. Ask questions. Always keep learning.

 Instead of thinking "I can't buy that because I don't have enough money," ask yourself different questions, such as: "What do I need to do to earn more money so I have enough?" "What do I have to offer others?" "Who do I know that can help me achieve my goal?"

 The best way to earn money is to create something that people need or want. If you can help people solve problems, you will create value… and money always chases value.